"Life is not a spectator sport.... If you're going to spend your whole life in the grandstand just watching what goes on, in my opinion you're wasting your life."

— JACKIE ROBINSON

JACKIE ROBINSON

BY TONY DE MARCO

The Child's World

COVER PHOTO

Portrait of Jackie Robinson
©Bettmann/Corbis

Published in the United States of America by The Child's World®, Inc.
PO Box 326
Chanhassen, MN 55317-0326
800-599-READ
www.childsworld.com

Product Manager Mary Francis-DeMarois/The Creative Spark
Designer Robert E. Bonaker/Graphic Design & Consulting Co.
Editorial Direction Elizabeth Sirimarco Budd
Contributors Mary Berendes, Red Line Editorial, Katherine Stevenson, Ph.D.

The Child's World®, Inc., and Journey to Freedom® are the sole property
and registered trademarks of The Child's World®, Inc.

Library of Congress Cataloging-in-Publication Data
De Marco, Tony.
Jackie Robinson / by Tony De Marco.
p. cm.
Includes bibliographical references (p.) and index.
ISBN 1-56766-918-2
1. Robinson, Jackie, 1919-1972—Juvenile literature. 2. Baseball
players—United States—Biography—Juvenile literature. 3. Afro-American
baseball players—Biography—Juvenile literature. [1. Robinson, Jackie
1919–1972. 2. Baseball players. 3. Afro-Americans—Biography.] I. Title.
GV865.R6 D45 2001
796.357'092—dc21

00-011739

Contents

Humble Beginnings

Coach Branch Rickey had just begun his lifelong career in baseball when he witnessed an event that changed his future—and the future of the game. The year was 1904. Rickey was coaching baseball at Ohio Wesleyan University. All the players on his team where white —except one, a first baseman named Charlie Thomas. The team was on a road trip to Notre Dame University for a game. They needed a place to stay, but the clerk at a hotel refused to let Thomas stay there because he was black. This was a common act of **discrimination** at the time.

Rickey did not want the team to find another hotel. He talked the hotel manager into putting a cot in Rickey's room for Thomas. Later that night, Rickey watched as Thomas sat on the cot and cried. Thomas rubbed his hands together as if he were trying to wipe off his black skin. He said aloud that he wished his skin were white. From that point on, Rickey promised to do whatever he could to prevent others from having to feel the way Thomas felt that night.

More than 40 years later, Rickey still thought about Thomas. He believed the time had come to end **segregation** in major league baseball. By then, Rickey was general manager of the Brooklyn Dodgers. At the time, none of the 16 major league teams had any black players. Rickey was going to change that, but to make history he needed just the right player. His search led him to Jackie Robinson. After one year in the minor leagues, Robinson stepped onto a major league diamond for the first time on April 15, 1947.

Beginning that day, baseball would never be the same. Many white fans taunted Jackie. Players from other teams were unkind to him as well. But black fans adored him. Everywhere Jackie played, fans went to ballparks to witness history. And everybody in America was watching the "great experiment" to see whether Jackie could handle the pressure. He did, opening the door for blacks and other minority players who have followed.

Ohio Wesleyan University

BRANCH RICKEY (SECOND ROW, FAR RIGHT) COACHED THE 1904 OHIO WESLEYAN UNIVERSITY BASEBALL TEAM. AS HE WATCHED THE TEAM'S ONLY BLACK PLAYER (CHARLIE THOMAS, STANDING AT CENTER) FACE DISCRIMINATION, RICKEY VOWED TO DO WHAT HE COULD TO FIGHT RACISM. MANY YEARS LATER, AS GENERAL MANAGER OF THE BROOKLYN DODGERS, HE BRAVELY OPENED MAJOR LEAGUE BASEBALL TO AFRICAN AMERICAN PLAYERS.

For a man who would help change an entire nation's view of his race, Jack Roosevelt Robinson had a humble beginning. He was born on January 31, 1919, in a cabin in Cairo, Georgia. He was the last of five children born to Jerry and Mallie Robinson. Jackie's parents worked as **sharecroppers** on the farm of a white landowner. It was a tough life, and the family had very little. Jerry Robinson left his family shortly after Jackie was born. He said he was going to find another job, but he never returned. He left Mallie to raise the children by herself.

At that time, acts of **racism** were common throughout the southern United States. Churches that black people attended were burned. Whites used threats to stop blacks from voting. Blacks could not attend the best schools or work at the best jobs. Worst of all, blacks often were victims of violence. Slavery had been outlawed for almost half a century, but African Americans were hardly free. Most opportunities for a good life were not available to them.

Mallie Robinson couldn't make enough money living on the farm. She decided to accept an offer from her brother, Burton, to move into his home in Pasadena, California. In May of 1920, Mallie and her children boarded a train and made the move west. At the time, Jackie was only 16 months old. He had three older brothers, Edgar, Frank, and Mack, and one older sister, Willa Mae.

In Pasadena, Mallie worked doing laundry for other families. Two years after the move from Georgia, she was able to buy a small house on Pepper Street. Living in a mostly white neighborhood, the family still faced **prejudice.** Blacks were allowed to use the YMCA pool only once a week. At local movie theaters, blacks could sit only in the balcony. Those acts of discrimination made Jackie angry. As a young boy, he promised himself that he would fight them one day. Little did he know what a difference he would make.

JACKIE ROBINSON WAS BORN IN THE TOWN OF CAIRO, GEORGIA, SHOWN ABOVE. BUT WHEN HE WAS STILL A BABY, HIS MOTHER TOOK HER FIVE CHILDREN TO LIVE IN CALIFORNIA.

THE MAN IN THIS PHOTOGRAPH IS DRINKING FROM A WATER JUG FOR "COLORED PEOPLE."
AFRICAN AMERICANS FACED PREJUDICE AND SEGREGATION ALL OVER THE UNITED STATES,
NOT JUST IN THE SOUTH. YOUNG JACKIE ROBINSON HOPED HE WOULD HAVE THE CHANCE
TO FIGHT RACISM ONE DAY.

Jackie's family was very close. He was proud of how his mother was raising the children by herself. But with his mother working most of the day, Jackie was on his own a lot. He began to get into trouble. For a while, he was a member of the Pepper Street Gang. He and his friends stole fruit and golf balls and did other mischievous things. They often had to report to a youth officer with the Pasadena Police Department. But two men took an interest in Jackie. They convinced him to quit the gang and stay out of trouble. One was Carl Anderson, a mechanic in the neighborhood. The other was Reverend Karl Downs, the pastor of Scott's Methodist Church.

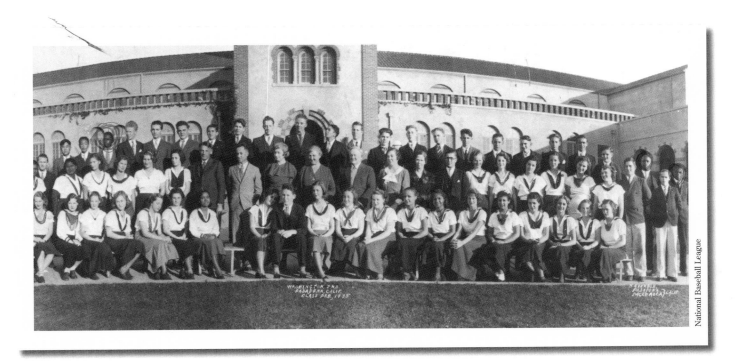

National Baseball League

JACKIE (STANDING AT FAR RIGHT) IS SHOWN HERE WITH HIS CLASS AT WASHINGTON JUNIOR HIGH SCHOOL IN PASADENA. SOMETIMES JACKIE GOT INTO TROUBLE AS A YOUNG BOY, BUT SUPPORT FROM HIS FAMILY AND FRIENDS HELPED HIM GROW INTO A RESPONSIBLE STUDENT AND A STAR ATHLETE.

A Skilled Athlete

As a teenager, Jackie turned his attention to playing sports. He found that he excelled at them. He enrolled at Muir Technical High School in Pasadena in 1933. There he played football, basketball, and baseball. Jackie also was part of the track-and-field team. He earned awards in all four sports. Baseball and track both took place in the spring, but that didn't stop him from participating. He simply split his time between the two.

Even though Jackie was a star in all four sports, he wasn't offered a **scholarship** to a big university. Instead, he enrolled at Pasadena Junior College in 1937. His older brother, Mack, had gone to school there. Mack also was an excellent athlete. In fact, he won a silver medal in the 200-meter dash at the 1936 Olympic Games in Berlin, Germany. Mack finished second behind another African American, Jesse Owens. In his day, Owens was called "the world's fastest human."

Jackie suffered a broken ankle during the football season at Pasadena Junior College. But he returned to lead the team to a 5–1 record. Then he led the basketball team in scoring. He also played shortstop on the baseball team and competed in the long jump for the track team.

One spring day during his second year at Pasadena Junior College was perhaps the best day in Jackie's **amateur** career. In the morning, he competed in a track meet and set a state record with a long jump of 25 feet, $6\frac{1}{2}$ inches. Then he drove 40 miles to help his baseball team win the Southern California Junior College Baseball tournament.

After his second year at Pasadena Junior College, Jackie was voted most valuable player in the Southern California Junior College Baseball League. His athletic successes there brought him several scholarship offers from four-year universities.

University of California, Los Angeles

JACKIE'S ATHLETIC TALENT EVENTUALLY EARNED HIM A SCHOLARSHIP TO ONE OF THE BEST UNIVERSITIES IN THE STATE—THE UNIVERSITY OF CALIFORNIA AT LOS ANGELES.

Bettmann/Corbis

JACKIE'S BROTHER MACK (AT LEFT) CAME IN SECOND IN THE 200-METER DASH AT THE 1936 OLYMPICS. HE SHOWED JACKIE THAT SPORTS WERE A WAY TO ACHIEVE SUCCESS. THE WINNER OF THE GOLD MEDAL WAS JESSE OWENS, SHOWN AT RIGHT.

Jackie wanted to stay close to home, so he accepted an offer from the University of California at Los Angeles (UCLA). Unfortunately, Jackie's family suffered a tragedy at about that time. His older brother, Frank, who had always supported Jackie's athletic career, died in a motorcycle accident.

At UCLA, Jackie continued to play football, basketball, baseball, and track. He became the first athlete to win **varsity letter** awards in all four sports. Even though Jackie's professional success came later in baseball, some people believe he was even better at the other sports. As a football running back, he had touchdown runs of 65 and 80 yards in his first year, before suffering another injury. He returned despite the setback to play in the final three games. He was named an All-American as a senior and traveled to Chicago and Hawaii to play in all-star games. In basketball, Jackie was the leading scorer in the Pacific Coast Conference for two years in a row. And in track, he won the national championship in the long jump.

In 1940, when Jackie was a senior at UCLA, he met Rachel Isum, a first-year nursing student. The couple would be married six years later, just before the beginning of Jackie's baseball career with the Brooklyn Dodgers.

AT PASADENA JUNIOR COLLEGE AND UCLA, JACKIE PLAYED FOOTBALL, BASKETBALL, AND BASEBALL. HE WAS ALSO PART OF THE TRACK-AND-FIELD TEAMS.

Pasadena City College

Despite his athletic successes at UCLA, Jackie decided not to play baseball and track in his senior year. Instead, he left school before graduating. He believed a college education offered no guarantee that a black man could find a good job. He also wanted to earn money to help his mother.

Jackie went to work as an athletic director for the National Youth Administration, which ran camps for kids. He also played semi-pro football for the Honolulu Bears. But at about that time, a history-making event occurred in Hawaii. The Japanese bombed Pearl Harbor on December 7, 1941. This act forced the United States to enter World War II. It also changed the direction of Jackie's life. Shortly afterward, he was **drafted** into the United States Army.

University of California, Los Angeles

AT UCLA, JACKIE BECAME KNOWN AS ONE OF THE BEST COLLEGE ATHLETES IN THE COUNTRY. HE LED THE LEAGUE IN SCORING WHILE ON THE BASKETBALL TEAM AND WAS AN ALL-AMERICAN RUNNING BACK IN FOOTBALL. IN TRACK AND FIELD, JACKIE EVEN BROKE HIS OLDER BROTHER MACK'S NATIONAL RECORD IN THE BROAD JUMP.

THE 1940 UCLA BASEBALL TEAM. JACKIE (STANDING AT FAR LEFT) QUIT COLLEGE IN HIS SENIOR YEAR BEFORE GRADUATION. IT WAS A DIFFICULT DECISION, BUT HE DID NOT THINK A COLLEGE DEGREE WOULD HELP HIM FIND EMPLOYMENT. "NO AMOUNT OF EDUCATION WOULD HELP A BLACK MAN GET A JOB," JACKIE LATER EXPLAINED. "I FELT I WAS LIVING IN AN ACADEMIC AND ATHLETIC DREAM WORLD."

Breaking Down Barriers

Jackie was assigned to Fort Riley, Kansas, for basic training. Unfortunately, he was the victim of more acts of discrimination and racism during his time in the service. After basic training, Jackie wanted to enroll in Officer's Candidate School. This program trained soldiers to become leaders in the military. But he and other African Americans who wanted to enroll were turned down. Jackie was angered by the decision. Seeking help, he talked to boxer Joe Louis, the world heavyweight champion. Louis also was stationed at Fort Riley, and he talked to military officials. Eventually, Jackie and other black soldiers were admitted into the officer's school.

Jackie became a second lieutenant in 1943, but that didn't end the discrimination. He began practicing with the Fort Riley football team. Jackie quit when he learned that he couldn't play against the University of Missouri team, whose members refused to play against blacks. Jackie also wanted to play for Fort Riley's baseball team but was told that he couldn't because he was black.

In 1944, Jackie was transferred to Fort Hood in Texas. There he ran into more racial trouble. One night, he was returning to the base by bus. He was talking to the wife of a white lieutenant. The bus driver ordered Jackie to move to the back of the bus, where blacks were expected to sit. Jackie refused to do so. Joe Louis and another boxer, Ray Robinson, had had similar experiences. Jackie knew that the army had banned segregated seating on buses. But when he got back to the base, he was still arrested. He faced a military trial for disobeying orders. Because segregated seating was against the army's rules, Jackie was found innocent. Finally, in November of 1944, he was allowed to leave the army. He never had to go to war.

National Baseball League

IN MARCH OF 1942, JACKIE WAS DRAFTED INTO THE
U.S. ARMY AND SENT TO FORT RILEY, KANSAS, FOR
BASIC TRAINING. UNFORTUNATELY, HE FACED PREJUDICE
AND SEGREGATION IN THE MILITARY.

The following spring, Jackie signed a contract to play with the Kansas City Monarchs. This team was part of baseball's Negro Leagues. Black players weren't allowed in the major leagues, so the first of the Negro Leagues was formed in 1920. Some of its best players were certainly good enough to play in the major leagues, including pitcher Satchel Paige, catcher Josh Gibson, outfielder Monte Irvin, and others. But instead, they had to play for low wages and put up with the poor travel conditions and fields in the Negro Leagues. Often, the players would have to sleep on their team bus because they were refused hotel rooms. They were refused food service from whites-only restaurants, too.

That same season, Branch Rickey of the Brooklyn Dodgers sent his **scouts** to watch the Negro League teams very closely. Publicly, Rickey said he was planning to start a Negro League team that would play in Brooklyn while the Dodgers were on the road. But secretly, he was planning to use one player to break the "color line" and become the first African American to play major league baseball. Rickey had specific ideas about the kind of player he wanted. He needed a player with not only great athletic ability but also exceptional intelligence, character, and courage. Several Negro League players were talented enough to play in the major leagues. But Rickey chose Jackie Robinson for his team.

Bettmann/Corbis

HEAVYWEIGHT BOXING CHAMPION JOE LOUIS (RIGHT) USED HIS POPULARITY TO GET JACKIE (LEFT) AND OTHER AFRICAN AMERICAN SOLDIERS ADMITTED TO OFFICER'S CANDIDATE SCHOOL.

Library of Congress

In 1945, Jackie signed a contract to play with the Kansas City Monarchs, part of baseball's Negro Leagues. Branch Rickey discovered Robinson while the future baseball star was playing for the Monarchs.

NBL/AP/WideWorld

JACKIE ROBINSON SIGNED A CONTRACT TO PLAY WITH THE MONTREAL ROYALS ON OCTOBER 23, 1945. HE WOULD SOON BECOME THE FIRST AFRICAN AMERICAN TO PLAY MAJOR LEAGUE BASEBALL. SEATED NEXT TO HIM IS BRANCH RICKEY, GENERAL MANAGER OF THE BROOKLYN DODGERS.

Near the end of the 1945 season, Rickey sent his scout, Clyde Sukeforth, to bring Robinson back to Brooklyn. He wanted to meet him face to face. Jackie and Rickey met for three hours on August 28. Jackie thought the meeting was going to be about playing for the new Black Dodgers team. But Rickey told him something else. He said he wanted Jackie to play for the real Dodgers. He warned Jackie that he would face racist comments and insults. Worse, he might even face death threats. He said Jackie wouldn't be permitted to fight back or even speak out against the attacks.

Jackie said, "Mr. Rickey, do you want a Negro player who is afraid to fight back?" And Rickey responded, "I want a player with the guts *not* to fight back." Rickey knew he had the right man for the job. On October 23, 1945, Jackie Robinson signed a historic contract to play the 1946 season with the Montreal Royals.

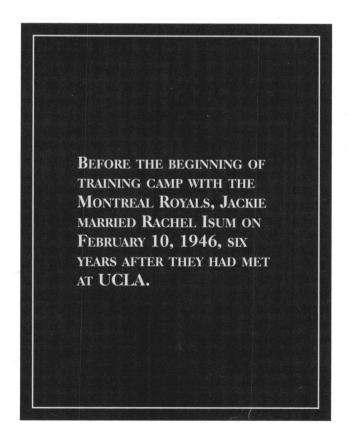

BEFORE THE BEGINNING OF TRAINING CAMP WITH THE MONTREAL ROYALS, JACKIE MARRIED RACHEL ISUM ON FEBRUARY 10, 1946, SIX YEARS AFTER THEY HAD MET AT UCLA.

Archive Photos

Baseball's First Negro

The Dodgers sign Jackie Robinson—first breach in game's racial barrier

John Roosevelt (Jackie) Robinson, 26-year-old former Army lieutenant and star four-letter athlete at UCLA (University of California in Los Angeles), recently became the first Negro player in the history of organized baseball.

A shortstop, Robinson was signed to an organizational contract by Branch W. Rickey, president of the Brooklyn Dodgers, and ordered to report next February to that club's principal minor-league affiliate, the Montreal Royals of the International League. Before the 1946 season is over Robinson may be in the Dodgers' line-up at their regular shortstop.

In signing Robinson, and several other Negro stars soon after, the Dodgers climaxed a $25,000, three-year scouting search under Rickey's direction throughout the United States and Latin America. They came up with baseball's first honest answer to the vital racial problem it had long evaded and other major-league teams were expected to follow their lead.

The real purpose behind the quest for Robinson and the other Negro stars was shrouded in deep secrecy. Until a month ago, even Brooklyn scouts believed they were seeking material to stock the Brown Dodgers, an All-Negro team Rickey has projected. **(Continued on next page)**

Robinson's speed, shiftiness delighted Pacific Coast football fans, sparked UCLA to undefeated 1939 season. Here he is in action against Southern California.

On a mediocre team, he led Pacific Coast Conference basketball scorers.

In track, Jackie won national-collegiate broad jump with 25-foot leap.

Twenty-six-year-old Jackie Robinson is intelligent, even-tempered, courageous, zealous to help his race.

IT WASN'T EASY TO PLAY FOR THE ALL-WHITE MONTREAL ROYALS. JACKIE FACED OPPOSITION FROM COACHES, OTHER PLAYERS, AND WHITE FANS. EVEN SO, HE MANAGED TO LEAD THE INTERNATIONAL LEAGUE IN BATTING AND RUNS SCORED. HE ALSO HELPED HIS TEAM WIN THE LEAGUE CHAMPIONSHIP. MAGAZINES AND NEWSPAPERS BEGAN TO WRITE STORIES ABOUT HIM, LIKE THE ONE SHOWN AT LEFT.

The Royals were the Dodgers' top **farm team.** The contract called for an award of $3,500 plus a monthly salary of $600. This was a big raise in salary from Jackie Robinson's Negro League days. But in exchange, Jackie had to face a great deal of public attention. When the contract was made public, the reaction was strong. Some people thought it was a great idea and long overdue. Other people were outraged. Would Jackie be able to **integrate** baseball? Was he good enough to make it to the major leagues? Everybody was eager to find out.

The Dodgers' training camp that season was in Florida, which still had segregation laws. Jackie again faced acts of discrimination, such as not being allowed to play in some teams' ballparks. Even his manager, Clay Hopper, didn't want him on the team.

Hopper asked Rickey to place Jackie on a different team, but Rickey refused. Still, once Hopper was forced to have Jackie on his team, he never showed any racism toward him.

Early in training camp, Jackie developed a sore arm and didn't play as well as he usually did. Some people wondered whether he would ever measure up. But once the regular season began, Jackie improved. Soon he began to excel.

The Royals' first game was against the Jersey City Giants on April 18, 1946. The game was played near New York City, and thousands of people showed up to watch the beginning of what many called the "great experiment." Jackie batted second in the game. He hit a ground ball to the shortstop in his first at-bat. But on his next at-bat, he belted a three-run home run. He circled the bases with a smile on his face. In the fifth inning, he laid down a bunt single and then showed the kind of baserunning that would become his trademark. He stole second base and moved to third on a groundout. Then he danced far off third base and caused the pitcher to **balk** in a run.

Jackie finished his first game with four hits in five at-bats, four runs scored, three RBIs (runs batted in), and two stolen bases.

With Jackie leading the way, the Royals quickly proved to be the best team in the International League. They easily finished in first place. Jackie became a fan favorite in Montreal. Still, he faced more racist attacks in opposing ballparks. A Syracuse player threw a black cat on the field, yelling to Jackie that the cat was his cousin. Jackie was also harshly taunted in Louisville during the Little World Series, which matched the winners of the International League and the American Association.

These attacks bothered Jackie. In Louisville, he had only one hit in three games. But when the Royals returned to Montreal to complete the series, the crowd cheered Jackie. The Royals won the final three games to take the championship. After the final victory, celebrating fans carried Jackie off the field. The "great experiment" had been a success so far. But Jackie's big step up to the major leagues was still to come.

Dodger Days

Before Jackie Robinson began his historic 1947 season, Rachel gave birth to their first child, Jackie Jr. Then Jackie was off to Havana, Cuba, for spring training with the Dodgers. Branch Rickey purposely moved training camp to the tiny island nation about 90 miles south of Florida. He hoped Jackie would be able to avoid the discrimination he would have faced in Florida. The idea was a good one. Jackie got off to a good start in spring training. He quickly proved that he belonged on the Dodgers' roster.

On April 10, Rickey made the decision to keep Jackie with the Dodgers. Hate mail arrived almost immediately from angry white fans. Some letters threatened Jackie with kidnapping or even death. But Jackie wasn't afraid. He started the regular season as the Dodgers' first baseman. One month into the season, the St. Louis Cardinals decided they didn't want to play against Jackie. But the president of the National League, Ford Frick, said he would suspend anyone who refused to play. The Cardinals finally backed down, and the games against Jackie and the Dodgers were played without any problems.

Boston Braves fans and players also **harassed** Jackie before one game. But when Dodgers shortstop Pee Wee Reese, a white player from the South, put his arm around Jackie's shoulder, the insults stopped. Jackie always remembered Reese's act of kindness. And Pee Wee always remembered Jackie. "Thinking about the things that happened," Pee Wee once said, "I don't know any other ball player who could have done what he did. To be able to hit with everybody yelling at him. He had to block all that out, block out everything but this ball that is coming in at a hundred miles an hour.… To do what he did has got to be the most tremendous thing I've ever seen in sports."

Library of Congress

BREAKING BASEBALL'S COLOR LINE WAS NOT EASY, BUT JACKIE ROBINSON FACED THE TASK WITH COURAGE. "I'M NOT CONCERNED WITH YOUR LIKING OR DISLIKING ME," HE SAID. "ALL I ASK IS THAT YOU RESPECT ME AS A HUMAN BEING."

Bettmann/Corbis

JACKIE ROBINSON IS SHOWN HERE WITH OTHER DODGER INFIELDERS BEFORE HIS FIRST GAME WITH THE TEAM. FROM LEFT TO RIGHT ARE SPIDER JORGENSEN, PEE WEE REESE, AND ED STANKY. PEE WEE REESE DID WHAT HE COULD TO MAKE JACKIE'S FIRST DAY AS A DODGER A LITTLE EASIER. THE TWO MEN BECAME GOOD FRIENDS.

Despite all the insults and harassment, Jackie had a great season. He was named National League Rookie of the Year. He batted .297 and led the league with 29 stolen bases and 125 runs scored. Brooklyn won the National League **pennant** for the first time in six years. Unfortunately, the Dodgers lost to their cross-town rivals, the New York Yankees, in the World Series.

Jackie made the mistake of starting his second season overweight. He got off to a bad start but finished strong, ending up with a .296 batting average. More important, Jackie's pioneering effort had paved the way for more black players in the game. Larry Doby came up to the majors with Cleveland halfway through the 1947 season to become the second black player in the majors and the first in American League history. Then the Dodgers signed four more African American players: Dan Bankhead, Don Newcombe, Roy Partlow, and Roy Campanella. By 1949, four blacks —Robinson, Campanella, Doby, and Newcombe—would play in baseball's mid-season All-Star Game.

Bettmann/Corbis

IT DIDN'T TAKE LONG FOR FANS TO EMBRACE JACKIE ROBINSON. HE PROVED HIMSELF TO BE AMONG THE VERY BEST PLAYERS IN MAJOR LEAGUE BASEBALL. THE "GREAT EXPERIMENT" WAS A SUCCESS.

Jackie's third season was the best in his 10 years in the major leagues. He was voted the National League's Most Valuable Player for 1949. He led the league with a .342 batting average and 37 stolen bases. He also set career highs with 122 runs scored, 124 RBI, 203 hits, 593 at-bats, and 12 triples. He was the league's most exciting base runner. The Dodgers won their second National League pennant in three seasons but again lost to the New York Yankees in the World Series.

By Jackie's fourth season, Branch Rickey finally allowed him to fight back at those who tried to hurt him. Rickey also allowed him to argue with umpires. Jackie, who switched to second base, continued his strong play. He finished the season with a .328 batting average and was the best second baseman in the National League.

The year 1950 brought important events off the field. Jackie and Rachel's only daughter, Sharon, was born. Jackie also starred in a movie about his life, *The Jackie Robinson Story*. It was filmed before the start of the 1950 baseball season.

But racism remained a problem for Jackie, even though he was in his fourth season in the major leagues. He received a serious death threat while the Dodgers were playing in Cincinnati that season. Nothing happened, and Jackie hit a game-winning home run that day. But the year ended on a bad note for Jackie when Branch Rickey left his job.

The 1951 season was another outstanding one for Jackie, but it also brought more disappointment. It was a tough year for the Dodgers, who again finished their season with a crushing loss. On the final day of the regular season, Jackie hit a game-winning home run to help the Dodgers reach the playoff for the National League pennant. The three-game playoff series with the New York Giants would go down as one of the greatest ever played. The two teams split the first two games. Then the Giants won the third game—and the series—on a dramatic three-run homer by Bobby Thomson.

Corbis

JACKIE WON THE NATIONAL LEAGUE'S MOST VALUABLE PLAYER AWARD IN 1949. THIS WAS THE BEST OF HIS 10 SEASONS IN MAJOR LEAGUE BASEBALL.

Corbis

The Dodgers won another National League pennant in 1952. Jackie did his part by batting .308 with 19 home runs, 75 RBI, 104 runs, and 24 stolen bases. But the Dodgers again lost to the Yankees in the World Series. The story was much the same in 1953, Jackie's last outstanding season. He batted .329 with 95 RBI and 109 runs, leading the Dodgers to the pennant. But the Yankees defeated them once again. The Dodgers would have to wait two more seasons before they could celebrate a World Series title.

Jackie's last two major-league seasons were troubled by injuries. He played fewer games and batted below .300 for the first time since his second season.

But the 1955 season finally brought a World Series championship when the Dodgers beat the Yankees. After the 1956 season, the Dodgers made a stunning announcement: they were moving across the country from Brooklyn to Los Angeles. They also decided to trade Jackie to the Giants, who were moving from New York to San Francisco. The Giants wanted Jackie to play for them and help tutor their young black star, Willie Mays. But Jackie didn't want to play for any team except the Dodgers. He decided to retire and never played another game in the majors. He finished with a career batting average of .311, 137 home runs, 734 RBI, 1,518 hits, and 197 stolen bases.

IN 1956, JACKIE ROBINSON PAID HIS LAST VISIT AS A DODGER TO
EBBETS FIELD, WHERE HE HAD PLAYED PROFESSIONAL BASEBALL
FOR THE LAST 10 YEARS. HE TOLD REPORTERS THAT HE WOULDN'T
PLAY BASEBALL AGAIN "FOR A MILLION DOLLARS." JACKIE WAS READY
TO DEVOTE HIS TIME TO OTHER INTERESTS.

Gone but Not Forgotten

Jackie quickly adapted to life after baseball. He was interested in both business and politics and got involved in several projects. He was named vice president of the Chock Full O' Nuts restaurant chain and took an active role in the company's management. Jackie also continued to be involved in the **Civil Rights Movement** to improve conditions for blacks. He wrote a newspaper column. He was an assistant to New York governor Nelson Rockefeller, working on civil rights issues.

Jackie's last major accomplishment in baseball came five years after he retired, when he was the first African American player elected to the Baseball Hall of Fame. The ceremony took place on July 23, 1962, in Cooperstown, New York. In his acceptance speech, Jackie thanked Branch Rickey for his courage. He also thanked his former teammates for their support.

But life after that brought some deep disappointments for Jackie. His son Jackie Jr. was wounded in the Vietnam War. After Jackie Jr. left the military, he was arrested for drug use. He eventually overcame his **addiction** and helped other people with similar problems. But in 1971, Jackie Jr. died suddenly in a car accident. He was only 24 years old.

Only a few months before his own death, Jackie Sr. attended a ceremony at Dodger Stadium in Los Angeles to honor the 25th anniversary of his breaking the color line. By then, he was suffering from health problems. He had lost most of his eyesight. On October 24, 1972, only 16 months after the death of his son, Jackie Robinson suffered a heart attack in his Stamford, Connecticut, home and died at age 53.

National Baseball League

More than 2,500 people attended Jackie's funeral at Riverside Church in New York City. In the **eulogy,** Reverend Jesse Jackson said, "Today we must balance tears of sorrow with tears of joy. When Jackie took the field, something reminded us of our birthright to be free." Jackie Robinson's impact on society is still remembered and honored today.

AT JACKIE ROBINSON SR.'S FUNERAL, REVEREND JESSE JACKSON (CENTER) SAID THAT ROBINSON DID NOT INTEGRATE BASEBALL FOR HIMSELF, BUT FOR ALL AFRICAN AMERICANS.

Timeline

1919	Jack Roosevelt Robinson is born in Cairo, Georgia, on January 31.
1920	Robinson's mother and her five children move from Georgia to Pasadena, California.
1933	Robinson enrolls at Muir Technical High School, where he wins letter awards in baseball, basketball, football, and track.
1936	Mack Robinson, Jackie's older brother, wins a silver medal in the 200-meter dash in the Summer Olympics in Berlin, Germany. He finishes behind African American Jesse Owens.
1937	Jackie Robinson enrolls at Pasadena Junior College, where he leads the basketball, football, and baseball teams to championships. He also sets a California junior college record with a broad jump of 25 feet, 6½ inches.
1939	Robinson enrolls at the University of California at Los Angeles. He becomes the school's first letter winner in four sports: baseball, basketball, football, and track. He leads the basketball team in scoring two seasons in a row, is named an All-American halfback, and wins the national championship in the long jump.
1942	Robinson is drafted and serves in the U.S. Army.
1945	Robinson plays one season with the Kansas City Monarchs of professional baseball's Negro Leagues. On October 23, he signs a historic contract with the Montreal Royals, the top farm team of the Brooklyn Dodgers.

1946	Jackie Robinson marries Rachel Isum on February 10. He plays one season with the Royals, leading them to the Little World Series championship.
1947	On April 15, Robinson makes history by becoming the first African American to play in the major leagues. He goes on to lead the National League in stolen bases and win the league's Rookie of the Year award.
1949	Robinson enjoys the best season of his career, leading the National League in batting average and stolen bases and winning the league's Most Valuable Player award.
1950	Robinson stars in a film depicting his life, *The Jackie Robinson Story.*
1955	The Brooklyn Dodgers win the World Series.
1956	Robinson plays the last of his 10 seasons with the Dodgers. The team is then sold and moved to Los Angeles. Robinson is traded to the New York Giants but announces his retirement instead.
1957	Robinson joins Chock Full O' Nuts as vice president of community relations.
1962	Robinson is elected to the Baseball Hall of Fame.
1972	Jackie Robinson dies in Stamford, Connecticut, on October 24.

Glossary

addiction (uh-DIK-shun)
If people have an addiction, they have a habit they cannot break. Jackie Robinson Jr. had an addiction to drugs.

amateur (AM-uh-chur)
An amateur is someone who does something for pleasure, not for money. As a sports amateur, Jackie Robinson played for college teams.

balk (BALK)
When pitchers balk, they make an illegal motion while pitching. When a pitcher balks, the base runner gets to take a base.

**Civil Rights Movement
(SIV-el RYTZ MOOV-ment)**
The Civil Rights Movement was the struggle for equal rights for African Americans in the United States during the 1950s and 1960s. Jackie Robinson took part in the Civil Rights Movement.

discrimination (dis-krim-ih-NAY-shun)
Discrimination is the unfair treatment of people simply because they are different. Jackie Robinson faced discrimination because he was an African American.

drafted (DRAF-ted)
A person who is drafted into the military is required to join rather than signing up by choice. Jackie Robinson and many other people were drafted into the U.S. Army during World War II.

eulogy (YOO-luh-jee)
A eulogy is a speech or writing in praise of someone who has died. Reverend Jesse Jackson delivered the eulogy at Jackie Robinson's funeral.

farm team (FARM TEEM)
A farm team is made up of players preparing to play for a major league team. Jackie Robinson signed a contract to play for the Montreal Royals, the Dodgers' top farm team.

harassed (huh-RAST)
Being harassed means being bothered by repeated attacks or insults. Fans and other players often harassed Jackie Robinson.

integrate (IN-teh-grayt)
To integrate means to bring together people who have been kept apart, especially because of race. People wondered if Jackie Robinson would be able to integrate baseball.

Glossary

pennant (PEN-nent)
A pennant is a flag awarded to the winner of a sports championship. In 1947, the Brooklyn Dodgers won the National League pennant for the first time in six years.

prejudice (PREJ-uh-diss)
Prejudice is a negative feeling or opinion about someone without a good reason. Black Americans have often faced prejudice from whites.

racism (RAY-sih-zim)
Racism is the unfair treatment of people because of their race. Jackie Robinson experienced racism.

scholarship (SKOL-er-ship)
A scholarship is money awarded to a student to help pay for his or her education. Jackie Robinson received a scholarship to attend the University of California.

scouts (SKOWTZ)
In sports, scouts are people paid to find skilled players for a team. The Dodgers' general manager sent scouts to watch the Negro League teams.

segregation (seh-greh-GAY-shun)
Segregation is the practice of using laws to keep people apart. Segregation laws separated blacks and whites in the United States for many years.

sharecroppers (SHARE-krop-erz)
Sharecroppers are farmers who work on another person's farm and are paid with part of the crop in return. Jackie Robinson's parents were sharecroppers.

varsity letter (VAR-sih-tee LET-ter)
A varsity letter is awarded to a student for unusual achievement in athletics. Jackie Robinson was the first student at UCLA to win varsity letters in four sports.

Index

Further Information

Books and Magazines

Coombs, Karen Mueller. *Jackie Robinson: Baseball's Civil Rights Legend.* Springfield, NJ: Enslow Publishers, 1997.

Green, Carol. *Roy Campanella: Major League Champion* (Rookie Biographies). San Francisco: Children's Book Press, 1994.

Mandel, Peter. *Say Hey! A Song of Willie Mays.* New York: Jump at the Sun, 2000.

McKissack, Pat, Patricia McKissack, and Frederick McKissack. *Black Diamond: The Story of the Negro Baseball Leagues.* New York: Scholastic, 1998.

Santella, Andrew. *Jackie Robinson Breaks the Color Line* (Cornerstones of Freedom). Chicago: Childrens Press, 1996.

Shirley, David. *Satchel Paige* (Black Americans of Achievement). Philadelphia: Chelsea House, 1993.

Stole, Alfred. *Finding Buck McHenry.* New York: HarperTrophy, 1993.

Web Sites

Visit the Library of Congress Web site's tribute to Jackie Robinson:
http://memory.loc.gov/ammem/jrhtml/jrhome.html

Visit the Major League Baseball Web site's tribute to Jackie Robinson:
http://www.majorleaguebaseball.com/u/baseball/mlbcom/jackie/jackie.htm

Visit the Pasadena City College Web site about Robinson:
http://www.paccd.cc.ca.us/75th/alumni/robinson/robinson.html

Visit the Dodgers' Web sites:
http://www.dodgers.com/
http://www.brooklyn-dodgers.com/

Read the text of President Bill Clinton's speech at the Jackie Robinson 50th Anniversary ceremony on April 15, 1997:
http://www.utexas.edu/students/jackie/robinson/clinton.html

Visit the Web site of the National Baseball Hall of Fame:
http://baseballhalloffame.org/